Facebook Made Easy

A Quick-Start, Step-by-Step Guide to the World's most Popular Social Media Site

By Cindy Baccus

Owner, Outta the Box Marketing

Table of Contents

Getting Started

Welcome to Facebook

Congratulations on deciding to start a Facebook profile! One of the most important decisions you will have to make while putting together your profile is the email account you want connected to your Facebook account. You should choose an email account that is personal and you will be keeping for the long haul. Facebook will communicate to you through this email with notifications, Facebook updates, friend requests, password retrieval, and more.

Facebook requires you to create a login, password and complete personal information before they provide you with a profile.

Don't be alarmed by entering your birthday, because you can set your profile settings to keep your birthday hidden from the public, friends, and acquaintances. This is sometimes used to confirm your identity when you are locked out of your profile.

Facebook will take you through several steps to set up your profile and connect with your friends.

> Step 1: Find your friends
>
> Step 2: Fill out information
>
> Step 3: Add profile picture

There is one problem with the order that Facebook has prepared for setting up your profile. Why would you find your friends before you have filled in your profile information and added a photo? I believe there is a better and more logical way to begin and I'll share that with you here.

My suggestion is to 'skip' Step 1 and remember that you can always find your friends after your profile is complete and your photos uploaded.

Step 1: Find your friends – SKIP THIS STEP FOR NOW

Step 2: Enter your information

You can complete as much or as little of your personal information as is your preference. The more information you have inside your profile, the easier it is for your friends to locate YOU. For example, your best friend from High School can locate you easier if you have notated this as part of your information.

Step 3: Add a profile picture

Facebook does give you the option to upload a photo or take one with your webcam. The perfect profile image size is 180 pixels by 180 pixels, but you can upload any photo and Facebook will give you the option to edit the piece that shows in the profile box.

Remember that your profile image should be something that represents you and that your friends and family would recognize to be you. Your profile image is open to the public and can be seen by anyone who happens to come across your profile, even people you do not know and are not connected to you in any way.

Once you finish uploading your profile picture, Facebook will take you to the Welcome Page set up to help you grow your friends and complete your profile.

NOW is a great time to go back to [Step 1: Find Your Friends](). And you can do that from this page. NOTE: This page will disappear once Facebook believes you have grown your page enough to be successful. But you can find your friends at any time from your Timeline or your Newsfeed.

Welcome Page:

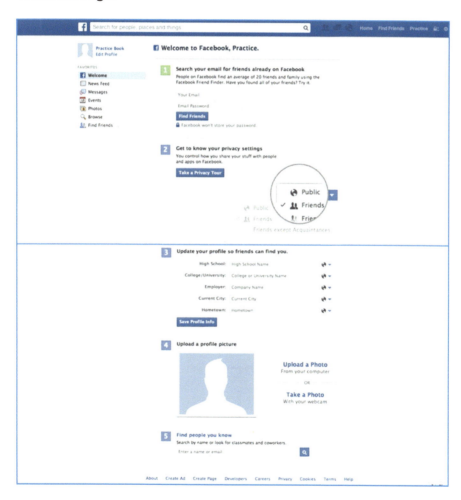

Privacy and Notification Settings

Ok, now that you have taken the first few steps to begin using Facebook let's talk about the privacy and notification settings now before you begin connecting to people.

Privacy settings are important for people who don't want their profile and posts to be completely public. If you have some doubt about allowing the world to see your activity on a daily basis, you need to continue reading this chapter. <u>Skip this chapter if you want your profile to be public and seen by the world</u>.

You can access the Privacy Settings through the lock icon that is located in the top right corner within the blue navigation bar. Click on 'See More Settings' located at the bottom of the box.

Ta da.....

The buttons on the left side will open to pages that correspond to Facebook privacy settings. The box on the right is the settings that correspond to the particular privacy issue.

Keep in mind that you can limit the public's access to your Facebook page and your activity on Facebook. The default setting is open to the public.

My suggestion is to click on each privacy line item and decide if that issue is important or not. For example...
Who can see my stuff? You can decide that only friends, friends of friends, or the public can see the posts and images you put on Facebook.
How much the world sees on your Facebook page is up to you.

Notifications are an important setting if you don't want to be bombarded with email notifications. You can set your Facebook notifications to only notify you when you login to Facebook or send you an email every time something happens. Your call!

The Timeline and Tagging page is important for you to review if you have Facebook friends that could possibly post inappropriate content on your timeline for everyone to see. (Maybe an old college picture you'd rather keep private?)

You can limit the posts that your friends and network make on your Timeline in this section. You can even approve items before they appear.

NOTE: Everyone can see your Timeline, but your News Feed is for your eyes only.

Timeline and Tagging

Tagging Review allows you to see any photo that you are tagged in before it is posted on your Timeline. You do have the ability to delete the photo from someone's timeline if you choose to once you review the tag.

Facebook will send you a notification anytime you are tagged in a photo and you must review it and approve it to be shown on your timeline.

YEAH, I look good! Or... Bad photo? No way, not on my Timeline!

Once you have finished setting up your privacy settings in a manner that is appropriate for you, it is best to then begin connecting to your friends and sending out some great updates.

What is a "Like", "Comment", and "Share"?

There are 2 **very** difficult pieces of Facebook to understand.

1. How much of my Facebook profile can the world see?
2. What is a "like", "comment", and "share" and where do they go when I click on them?

The world of Facebook is a giant spider web that changes every time they decide to update their system. Today you may feel blessed to keep up with the grandkids and watch what is happening in their lives and then tomorrow you find out all your personal photos are being added to a database Facebook uses for advertising. Ok, I don't want to scare you but you do need to understand that everything you do is being tracked and can be recalled when needed. What a world we live in today!

Let's talk about the Like, Comment, and Share options you see at the bottom of posts your friends and yourself have added to Facebook.

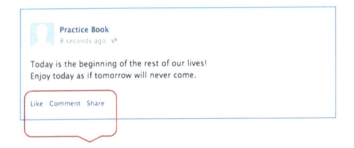

Like, Comment, Share
Found at the bottom of all posts

Every training I have ever conducted included the questions...

"What happens when I hit the 'like' button, post a comment, or share a post?"

"Who sees my comment?"

"Where does my 'share' go?"

"Can my Facebook friends see the posts that other friends send me?"

This is one of the hardest pieces of Facebook for everyone to really understand.   If you remember anything from this book, I hope that you remember this.

When you engage with posts on Facebook you are allowing other people to see your posts, profile, and activity on Facebook. Hitting the "Like" button, commenting on a post, or sharing a post allows your friends, friends of friends, and anyone else who receives the post to see your activity.

In the simplest of terms... always assume that unless you are writing on your own timeline, what you are doing is PUBLIC.

"Like"

Let us begin with the famous LIKE button. When you like a post you have now added your name to the post, a direct link to your profile, and a new listing to your activity log.

The Allen Americans' post below is a great example to help you understand the mass numbers of people who could get access to your name and profile.

The Allen Americans have 9,485 fans and they sent out the following post. The post received 51 shares, 303 likes, and 6 comments by the time I copied the post for the book.

When you hit the "Like" button your name has the potential of being seen by not only the entire fan base of Allen Americans, but anyone who received a shared post from the 51 people who shared the post. Wow! These numbers add up quickly.

Left: 303 people liked the post

Right: Clicking on the 303 people opens a window to show you who they are & direct link to their profile

"Comment"

Now that you understand the Like button we can talk about the Comment button. There will be times when you feel that your comment or thought would add to the original post and feel the need to hit the Comment button. Great!

Ray Charles The Golden Retriever page (below) is an excellent example to explain where your comment will go once you hit enter. The Ray Charles The Golden Retriever page has 98,472 fans, as of the day I am writing this book, and always has high engagement numbers with the posts they send out. The post below has 2,596 likes, 130 comments, and 44 shares. If we decided to hit the Comment button and post a thought the following would occur:

1. Your comment, photo, and name would be added to the post's comments for all their fans to see.
2. Your name would be a direct link back to your profile.
3. All the friends of the 44 sharers can see your comment, name, and direct link back to your profile.

Now, the friends of the 44 sharers **could** possibly share their friend's post and now even more people will see your comment. Just FYI... this number is not reflected within the Ray Charles The Golden Retriever statistics you see on the post.

Ray Charles The Golden Retriever – 98, 472 fans connected to this Page.

"Share"

So what happens if you hit the "Share" button instead of the "Comment" button?

The Share button is the most important button for your post to go viral. When you hit the Share button, you are sending the original post and a special message to your Facebook friends. If they like your post, then they can share your post with their friends and so on and so on. You have created several layers of friends from each share.

If you can create a post or image that people are connected to emotionally enough to share with their Facebook friends, your post may go viral.

Remember that if you share your friends' posts on a regular basis, they will share your posts with their friends if you send a great post. Do unto others as you would have others do unto you!

Toffee Treats &
Chocolate
Sweet's post

You are probably asking who will see your shared post? Your friends will be the first to see your name connected to the original post. This will be found on your Timeline so anyone who comes to your Timeline could actually see the post if you have your settings on public. Your name and direct link back to your profile will follow the post as it is shared among others.

Newsfeed vs Timeline

One of the most important features of your Facebook profile is your Timeline. This is the chronological history of your activity on Facebook. It will keep your personal posts, shared posts, and liked page activity accessible by date.

The Timeline is available to read by either the public, friends of friends, or friends. This is a setting you must change if you do not want the default of public accessibility.   Remember that your activity on Facebook could be seen by anyone who happens upon your profile and if you're fine with that, great! But just be sure to make the choice.

Timeline

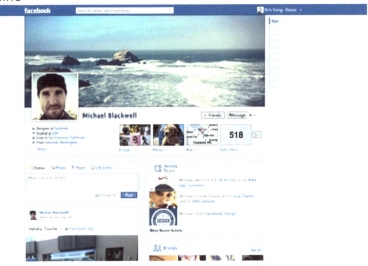

The Newsfeed is the inbound feed of your friends, business pages you have 'liked', and ads from businesses within your network. Your eyes only see this and no one has access to this information. So, if you have college students as friends and they are posting about the awesome parties they are attending while at college, your Facebook friends do not see their posts coming into your Newsfeed. But remember that if you Like, Comment, or Share one of their posts then your friends could potentially see your activity on that particular post.

Always remember that you should conduct yourself online in a way that is respectful of the personality and reputation you want the public to know and see. The Internet is a world filled with crawlers and searchers looking for the opportunity to share some data.

Newsfeed

Here's a great tip for anyone who doesn't want Facebook to decide what is important to you without asking you first.

Facebook has created an algorithm for your Newsfeed. It will not show every post from every friend and all the business pages you have 'liked' in the history of your Facebook. They have decided to send out only a small portion of the entire list of posts that you would be receiving if they did send the total amount of posts to you every day.

You have probably noticed that your Newsfeed is not in chronological order either. Facebook, once again, decides what is more important to you and moves it to the top of your Newsfeed and sends those posts they don't think you will enjoy to the bottom.

You are now wondering 'how the heck do they know what I enjoy and what I don't enjoy'? When you hit the 'like' button, decide to comment on a post, or 'share' a post with your friends, Facebook collects that information and makes a judgment call on the posts you receive on your Newsfeed from that activity.

You probably think that this doesn't seem to take your real interests into consideration. Maybe you enjoy reading posts more than actually engaging with them on your Newsfeed. You could be the person who doesn't share posts at all, but enjoys keeping up with your friends and family. Maybe you are following a business, but don't want anyone to know and therefore are not engaging with that business' posts.

Your activity and lack thereof is all taken in consideration when they decide what posts will come through into your Newsfeed and in what order.

Did you know that you **COULD** change your Newsfeed to run in chronological order?

Now please note that this has to be changed <u>every time</u> you enter your Facebook profile, because it will continue to change back into the default mode of 'Facebook's Importance Order.'   And FYI, it <u>cannot</u> be changed on your Facebook mobile app, as this works only on the desktop computer version.

To change your Newsfeed to chronological order follow the steps below.

> **Step 1:** While in Facebook you must be looking at your Newfeed page (not your Timeline)
>
> **Step 2:** Find the 'sort' button on the right top corner of your Newsfeed, but just below the status update box.
>
> **Step 3:** Click on the triangle just beside 'sort' and you should have 2 options. 'Top Stories' and 'Most Recent.'
>
> **Step 4:** Hover over the 'Most Recent' button and click to change your Newsfeed.

You can now verify at the top right corner of your Newsfeed that the 'sort' button reads 'sort: most recent' now. Congratulations! You are now receiving the posts in chronological order.

This does **NOT** mean that you are receiving **ALL** your friends' posts, business page posts, or advertising posts. Facebook still chooses which posts arrive in your Newsfeed, but you do get to read them in chronological order.

Posting on your Facebook Profile

Posting on your profile is fairly simple and you can do it from either your Timeline or your Newsfeed in the "Update Status" or simply "Status" box where it asks you…"What's on your mind?"…

In the images below you will see where these boxes appear at the top of the screen. This is where you can talk about what is literally "on your mind", you can post a picture or a video and you can share that information immediately.

There are a few important social etiquette rules you should remember when thinking about writing an update. Remember that just because you are sitting behind your computer or cell phone your face is not forgotten when your family, friends, peers, employees, or neighbors read your posts.

Social etiquette rules to consider:

1. The Facebook world does not want to hear your whining every day.
2. Choose images that are not going to offend young minds, because they are passed around the Facebook world.
3. Try not to spend too much time engaging with posts, sharing posts, and creating posts all at once. This could be considered spamming.
4. Imagine that your mother or father (or even grandmother!) will see your post.
5. Do not share nudity.

6. If you use profanity, remember that some profiles are blocking profanity and your posts will be blocked.
7. Promoting yourself or your business too often will create a flood of friends deleting your Facebook friendship.
8. Have fun! Social media has proven to be a great place for sharing success, celebrations, excitement, great stories, sad stories, and more.

Spend some time practicing your updates with links, photos, text, tagging, and videos. If you make a mistake there is a 'Delete' button that is always accessible to you. Enjoy reading, sharing, and engaging with your friends and favorite business pages on a regular basis. You may get some great ideas for new posts or something awesome to share.

Facebook SmartPhone Application:

The main reason you may want to set up a Facebook profile is to keep connected to your friends and family while you are moving around your regular daily life. You can put your friends at the heart of your phone. Glance at your phone for friends' updates and get notifications on your home screen.

Parents are waiting for their kids throughout the day and driving them to activities they are involved in. One hour is usually not enough time to run other errands so many parents will be seen scrolling through their smartphones, Ipads/Tablets, or Kindles while they wait for their kids.

You may have a job that entails you meeting current or prospective clients, or staff out of the office. Planning to arrive early to an appointment is of course the best plan, but this leaves you with extra time while you wait. What better use of your EXTRA time than to keep up with your friends and family on Facebook. You can easily click your exit button and be ready for your appointment when they arrive.

You will learn that the mobile app version of Facebook is not going to give you the same level of functionality that the computer desktop version does. Yes, it can be a bit of a pain when you spend most of your time on the mobile app version and want to complete specific tasks while you are using your mobile device, but the most important feature that you will use is the Newsfeed. Your connected friends and family posts, business page posts, and some advertising will arrive in your Newsfeed throughout the day. You can set your phone notifications to alert you when you have activity happening within your network. This can also be very annoying as you begin to gather more friends and more business pages, so adjust your settings according to your needs for notification.

How to Share Things with Your Friends

As you continue utilizing Facebook you will eventually come across an article, great recipe, funny video or some other interesting tidbit that you would like to share with your friends. Here are step-by-step instructions on how to post this information.

Step 1: Did you find an article, blog, or recipe that you would like to share on Facebook? Make sure you have one window open on your computer that includes what you want to share.

Step 2: Highlight the URL within the open window (that's the www…. address)

Step 3: Right click your mouse (or, hit 'control C' if you are a Mac user)

Step 4: Click 'copy'

Step 5: Open your Facebook window and login to your account.

Step 6: Click on 'What is on your mind' box located at the top of your page.

Step 7: Right click your mouse (or, hit 'control V' if you are a Mac user)

Step 8: Click 'paste' and watch Facebook pull in an image and title from the page you want to share.

Step 9: Once the image, title and short description has been pulled in by Facebook, you must delete the original URL that you pasted into the 'What is on your mind' box.

NOTE: The original URL will not delete once the new live link is available. You must delete the URL yourself.

Step 10: Type your fun message about why you want your friends to click on the link and read. Make it unique and fun!

Step 11: Click 'post!'

Awesome! Now you can share any information you come across on the Internet. Beware that sharing everything that you enjoy may not always be the best option. Remember that your friends don't always love the things you do, but it could also be something they enjoy when they do read it. Have fun searching the Internet.

Important Tips & Tricks

Now that you have prepared your profile and started connecting to family and friends, it is time you learned a few special tips and tricks.

Have you heard the saying, "There are no dumb questions?" You may encounter many questions once you really begin practicing your Facebook interactions. I have put together a few tips to help answer some questions that you probably have on your list. If the end of this book has not answered your questions, feel free to visit the Outta The Box Marketing Facebook Page and post your question or send a direct message to me on the Page.

How many of your friends actually see a post?
Facebook has published the average number of people who see an organic post to be on average 16%.

Can a person promote a post on their Facebook profile?
Facebook has given people the opportunity to promote posts on their personal page. A few great examples would be garage sales, emergency announcements, baby announcements, engagements, or non-profit fundraising posts.

Would you like to share a post with just one friend?
'Sharing' photos, videos, images, or other posts with individual Facebook friends can be achieved by clicking the 'on your own timeline' button (found at the top of the post) and choose 'on a friend's timeline.'

"Be careful with your words. Once they are said, they can only be forgiven, not forgotten."

Did you enjoy putting together your Facebook profile?

Connect with Outta The Box Marketing today to continue receiving updates and new tips & tricks in your email inbox, on Facebook, or your favorite social network.

Or...Do you want to set up Facebook page for your business? Outta The Box Marketing has a new book with Step-by-Step instructions as well as tips and tricks to help you set up your business page and learn how to engage with fans and customers. We understand that you don't have a lot of time to learn how to use social marketing when you are building your business. This is why we are creating Step-by-Step guides to help you with the pieces that interest you most.

You can register for the monthly newsletter that includes new announcements, social network updates, and fun videos that you can share with your fans.

Register today by:

     1. **Texting** OUTTATHEBOX to 22828

     2. **Or** scanning the **QR code** below and follow the directions sent to you.

Have fun with your newfound Facebook skills!

@OuttaTheBoxMktg

Facebook.com/OuttaTheBoxMarketing

YouTube.com/user/OuttaTheBoxMarketing

Linkedin.com/in/cindywatts9

Plus.google.com/+CindyBaccus

Xeesm.com/CindyWatts

A Publication of

www.OuttaTheBoxMarketing.com

www.ingramcontent.com/pod-product-compliance
Lightning Source LLC
Chambersburg PA
CBHW041148050326

40689CB00001B/532